Cozy Country Interiors

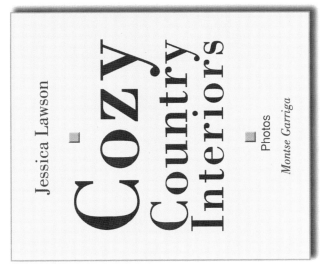

Jessica Lawson

Cozy Country Interiors

Photos
Montse Garriga

Author
Jessica Lawson

Photos
Montse Garriga

Texts
Eva Marín Quijada

Translation
Mark Holloway

Design and layout
Manel Peret Calderón

Image
Enric Navarro i Comas

Director of production
Juanjo Rodríguez Novel

Copyright © 2004 Atrium Group
Published by:

Atrium Group de ediciones y publicaciones S.L.
Ganduxer, 112
08022 Barcelona
Tel. +34 932 540 099
Fax: +34 932 118 139
e-mail: atrium@atriumgroup.org
www.atriumbooks.com

ISBN: 84-96099-38-5
Dep. Leg: B-19.967-2004

Printed in Spain
Ferré Olsina, S.L.

Summary

introduction

What is it that makes us feel so good in the country? Outside, in contact with nature, the vegetation and the exuberance of the landscape envelop us. More than ever, the house becomes a refuge that welcomes us and offers us shade and coolness in summer and the warmth of a home in winter. The following pages present an array of welcoming rustic corners and show us what the basic ingredients are that make us feel so comfortable in them.

In a certain way, a rural residence always has something of austerity about it because, far from competing with the richness of the natural environment, it is a place of rest and shelter. Why is it that some become cozy places where we meet with friends and family to share meals and experiences while in others, we never quite manage to feel at home? With dwelling places, we also establish relationships and, to a large extent, the secret of obtaining the atmosphere desired lies in substantiating our project and putting all of our care and attention into it. If we open ourselves to them, we will be constructing a home which, as to quote the Spanish writer Antonio Gala, "It is the house that awaits us". As with people, we should respect their character and draw out and strengthen their positive aspects. Beyond tendencies and fashions, it is fundamental to adapt them to our own style and endow them with accessories that have personality.

This book offers numerous suggestions on how to ease the task of dressing these spaces and giving them quality. A fundamental aspect that we find is the use of color, which goes beyond aesthetic tastes and affects us mentally. Earth colors are full of vitality and facilitate communication, creams are heart-warming, white is full of light and simplicity while indigo makes us dream. With a little dedication when it comes to designing the spaces and choosing the color scheme that we are going to use, according to whether we want a refuge in which to read or relax after a hard day's work or a place where we can merrily converse in company, we can make our home a small oasis.

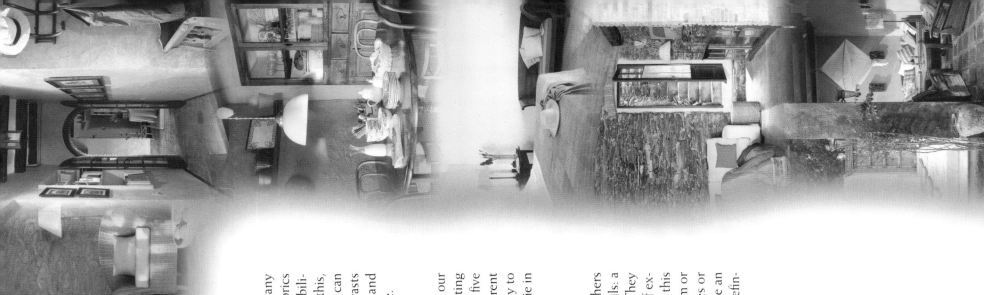

The materials used also constitute a fundamental aspect within any environment. Terracotta floors, wooden beams, forged steel and natural fabrics are a smart combination which balances the lightness of gauze with the stability of steel. The different textures of a room visually enrich the spaces. If, to this, we add the correct illumination, which varies over the length of the day, we can obtain true artistic compositions. They are these elements and the contrasts established among them that make us feel so comfortable among light and shade, soft cushions and solid structures, linen net curtains and living stone.

Also outside, inevitably, we humanize the landscape, we make it our own to enjoy the sensuality of spring from the garden while comfortably sitting on cushions below a pergola or under the shade of a grapevine. With our five senses, we relish each and every variation in light, each nuance of the different seasons. We conceive spaces in the open air which allow us certain intimacy to chat comfortably with family and friends around a table, or we can simply lie in a hammock and snooze wrapped up in the sounds of nature.

Those that follow are corners full of stories, some are real and others are fantasies, told in front of the fire over coffee or contained in small details: a portrait, a vessel, a mark upon the wall… they are, in some ways, timeless. They unify the past and the present and keep themselves away from fashion as if experience had given them wisdom. It is all the same what people are wearing this season. We can rescue some forgotten pieces of furniture from the storeroom or buy them from an antique dealer and mix them with other modern pieces or with everyday utensils. To create our own place in the world should not be an arduous task, but a cheering one which leads, in one way or another, to us defining our very selves and what we wish to transmit to others.

corners full of charm

It is the first impression that counts. As soon as we open the door we start to form an idea as to whether we are going to like the house or not. Is it hospitable? If we are welcomed by the first impression, it will be difficult for the rest to let us down. As far as

possible, the reception area should be in keeping with the overall tone of the home as it is going to be the first and last image that our visitors are going to have. The same applies to the passages and distribution areas. If we take care of the details and try to create a harmonious whole, the communication and fluidity between different areas will be favored.

Although these intermediary spaces are primarily transit areas, there is no reason why they should not be full of charm. Let's allow ourselves to be surprised by the white rabbit just as in Alice in Wonderland and discover that corner below the window in the corridor that seems to be made to measure for that old chair of grandmother's that, once reupholstered in eye-catching plaid, will become our favorite place to read. A space under the staircase can be an ideal place for a bookcase and, if, near by, there is enough space in which to put a winged armchair or a small writing desk, we can complete our study by converting into a useful zone that was initially no more than a transit area.

And why not allow ourselves to play a little? The old structures respond to necessities that have changed with the times. What was once destined to a storage area for tools and so on is now a beautiful hall. We can make the most of that space that came about from closing up the doorway to install built-in shelving. Fitted out with cushions, that step may make us just as comfortable as if we were sitting in a marvelous armchair. Rustic hallways tend to be roomy and are often large enough not only for decorative pieces, but for functional objects such as coat hangers and umbrella racks or even a small divan to sit upon while taking off those shoes or boots and coat after a walk in the country. If, in addition, we have picked a small bunch of wild flowers and we put them on the small table in the entrance, we will have filled the area with freshness and it will be in keeping with its surroundings.

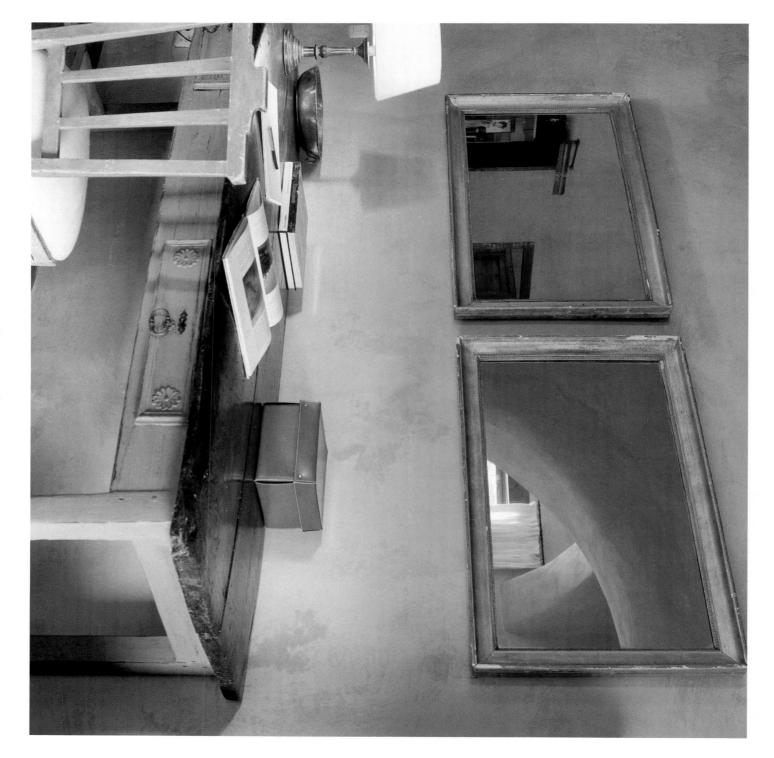

DRESSING THE SPACES

Transit areas run the risk of being insipid due to the fear of losing space. In these cases, pieces such as console tables are ideal accessories given that they occupy a small amount of space and can be used as writing desks. It is also quite simple to arrange a few books on top, a box in which to keep small bits and pieces or a lamp that can contribute to enriching the indirect lighting of the area.

A few well chosen pictures hung on the walls of a transit area give it personality.

THE MARK OF TIME

The beauty of this console table and the gilded frames of the mirrors lie, to a great extent, in the marks that the passing of time has left on them. On this piece of furniture, which fulfills the function of writing table, the marks have become transformed into landscapes over the varnished wood. It is just these small imperfections that we can see in the finishes of these pieces that represent added value and that let on about their authenticity, their lineage. In addition, the mirrors contribute to giving a sensation of amplitude. In spite of the rustic aspect of some of the finishes, the composition is elegant, thanks to the intervention of a few carefully chosen elements.

12

ARCHES AND STONE

The charm of these ambiences often lies in finding the right balance between the old structures and present-day elements. The stone walls combine to perfection with the natural colors that introduce luminosity to the setting. In the entranceway, in the image on the right, the best has been made of a series of arches, which originally corresponded to an exterior gallery by closing them off with glass in such a way as to convert them into a space for multiple use. In the top image, the simplicity of the forms and of the furniture complement each other with the great expressiveness that the contrast of lively colors brings.

ALL ABOUT MATERIALS

A few elements take on a great relevance in the setting. In this case, we could practically talk about monochromy as the small number of components that are involved blend into the walls of living stone. In front of this backdrop, an old wooden bench, a round auxiliary table with a small lamp and decorative accesories are the only elements that introduce a touch of color. Visually, the creation of a sensation of amplitude is achieved in the transit zone in which the usable surface area is made the most of without giving up comfort or functionality. It could be said that this comes from the influence of minimalism in the rustic style.

An Exotic Touch

The crimson red gives this space an oriental touch that is reinforced by the white net curtains that serve to separate the room from the landing.

The artisanal carpets on a wooden floor complete the exotic atmosphere of these areas.

On the following page, we can see how classical accessories for the reception area, a hat stand and umbrella rack, have been chosen.

The basket with flowers placed next to the red door gives a personal and informal touch to the overall scene.

SPACES FULL OF TEXTURES

In houses in the country, the finishes of the walls tend to be much richer: stone, rendered or bare brick take on a very different air when they are painted white. The result is a relaxed atmosphere in which decorative simplicity dominates. With no more than a few well-chosen bits and pieces a striking atmosphere full of light and texture is achieved. In the illustration on the right, for example, some straw hats and a deckchair take us off to small fishing villages on the coast. We can lie back in it and imagine that the breeze that is coming in through the window comes from a nearby sea.

WHITE LIGHT

The white walls and terracotta floors emphasize the rustic style of the home. In this case, a simple, almost spontaneous, decoration has been opted for. Some umbrellas with wooden handles, a picture, a basket with freshly picked flowers and a small lamp… objects that have a special value to the owners and which have and contain history.

On the stairs in the image on the right, a simple wooden stick has become an improvised hanger.

TO SEE BEYOND

It is not enough to look, you have got to be able to see. The old structures allow us to play with our imagination and to create new uses to make the most of each and every corner. In this case, some cushions convert this whitewashed brick dais next to the bookcase into an ideal place for reading. In addition, the shelving built into the wall reproduces the same volumes which balances the group. In this way, the use en masse of white gives greater luminosity to the area and produces a greater sense of space. Details such as the cushions in a toasted color, the books and a photograph fill this ambience, which is bathed with a generous amount of natural light, with warmth.

24

OLD AROMAS

A stone arch separates the two ambiences of the living room in which the lightness of the fabrics contrasts with the rustic furniture in wood. Some colorful carpets made from natural fibers manage to give a welcoming air to the setting given that, on occasions, floor tiles do not tend to give as much warmth as other materials. In rural houses, it is common to recondition old spaces that were once dedicated to activities related to working the land so as to increase, in this way, the usable surface area. In the image on the right, the rustic air has not only been conserved, but it has also been strengthened by the presence of the aromatic flowers hanging from the ceiling.

CORNERS TO DREAM IN

With the right mixture of styles we can create very suggestive spaces. A hollow under a window has been made the most of, for example, to position a saddari, a traditional Arabian sofa, which converts it into an ideal reading corner. The curtains accentuate the exoticism and are an invitation to fantasizing and play. A winged armchair and built-in shelving finish off this intimate and original space.

In the top photograph, in contrast, austerity and minimal decorative intervention have been preferred to allow the wood to stand out.

BLUE AND WHITE

The sun is a source of energy and vitality. If we dedicate a little time to studying all of the corners in the house, we are sure to discover places that are worth conditioning to make the most of natural light.

A large range of blues exist. Those which contain a greater quantity of red and tend towards lilac are not so cold. If, in addition to this, we select woods in light tones or lightly stained, we will achieve considerable effect with few elements.

FLUFFY TOYS AND PETS

We cannot forget that in the country we relate more to animals, with those with which we live on many occasions. Rustic houses are much more prepared for pets. The materials and the furniture do not tend to be so delicate, which allows us to go in and out with our loyal friends in a much more relaxed way.

walls that speak

These walls of stone eroded by time tell us so many stories.... They know all about our joys and worries and plans for the future. They are impregnated with conversations, laughter, consoling words. They see how the hours go by, the days, and the seasons, far removed from fashion, from the tones that are being worn, from tendencies. They harbor spaces with personality that wish to create atmospheres of serenity and warmth in which we can sit in comfort and where we hope others feel at home.

White or natural pigments on the walls? Both combine to perfection with the warm colors of the terracotta floors and steel or wooden beams. These elements constitute a good base on which to create a welcoming home. A selection of fabrics with character and some small details will do the rest. We can recover the old console table forgotten in the storage room, look for other furniture in the local flee market or choose select pieces from a good antique dealer. The important thing is to be faithful to our style and to make sure that everything fitts together. Some prefer to see the different areas develop in an organic way, after getting to know them, to living them. Others are delighted to sit down at a table and design, alone or in a group, every room to achieve the desired effect. Everything goes as long as you bear some fundamental aspects of decoration in mind.

The living room is the place where we meet with our own and, so that we feel comfortable, a careful distribution in which the volumes are well balanced in essential. The furniture may be heavy, but unless we want to darken the area excessively, we should opt for light tones. If there is little natural light, a selection of neutral colors will intensify what there is. The orientation of the living room will determine this aspect that is so fundamental; south and west are the best for enjoying the sun at midday or during the afternoon. In addition, these zones of daytime use tend to be those most open to the exterior by ways of doors and balconies. Frequently, the best work of art that can be exhibited is the natural landscape contained in the window frame.

MODERN OR CLASSIC

These two living rooms, in which contrasts of light and shade have been used en masse, present clearly differentiated styles. Conceptual art and objects with great distinction in one, in spite of its reduced dimensions, and a much clearer and classical ambience in the other, on the following page, in which an eclectic style has been chosen which mixes restored furniture and classical objects with present-day pieces.

PAST AND PRESENT

A wise balance of modern and classical elements and accessories will give a more adequate atmosphere for this kind of house in which wooden beams, vaulted structures and fired clay floors coexist with furniture of more contemporary lines. With the reinterpretation of old elements such as these seats, which have been upholstered in an electric blue microfiber, a much more up-to-date style has been achieved. In this way, some pieces of contemporary art may well become great allies, such as the abstract oil painting of large dimensions exhibited in this living room, in complete harmony with accessories of a more traditional line such as the lamp or small ceramic base over the occasional table.

NAUTICAL AMBIENCES

White, blue and sun. We can almost notice the smell of the sea that is breathed in this living room. These colors give a great freshness to the spaces as well as strengthening the luminosity.
Books, figurines, lamps and flowers, small pictures in different styles, no end of details and accessories that make us feel that they are family places which are full of life.

ARISTOCRATIC AIRS

When it came to decorating these two rooms, a style in keeping with that of the building itself was maintained. The austerity
in the decorative intervention along with the more up-to-date sofas, not to mention the colors used, manage to give
a contemporary touch to the whole. It is a warm elegant atmosphere in which a detail as simple as the worn leather
on the armchair brings a bohemian aspect into play which seems to talk to us about an aristocratic past.

STONE AND WHITENESS

A house in the country that is appreciated has to have a good fireplace for the long winter months and a large comfortable sofa with soft cushions close to the hearth. We do not need much more for the long hours of chatting, playing and reading. Stone, wood and iron or other metals are resistant materials and which, in turn, stand out and allow for a great variety of textures in our compositions.

ANCESTRAL CUSTOMS

Fire continues to exercise a strange fascination for human beings. We can spend hours observing the dancing flames, absorbed in the continual crackling. Who is interested in a television program if they can enjoy a live show? We should allow ourselves to be seduced by these spaces in which time seems to have been detained and recover ancestral customs such as the oral tradition. Transmitting family stories from generation to generation or inventing new tales in the warmth of the fireplace can turn out to be a real pleasure. The decorative simplicity is a great virtue, it allows for the creation of serene atmospheres that are open to contemplation or communication.

46

ORIENTAL AIRS

Small details often have the great quality of being able to change the atmosphere of a room. A few suggestive objects acquired on our travels in distant lands can transform a living room equipped with simple furniture into a warm room with an oriental touch. However, in the enormous global village in which we live, silk and gold cushions can be acquired without the necessity of travelling to India.

Earth colors are especially indicated for creating welcoming atmospheres. They combine to perfection with bare stone and lightly stained wood. With finishes of this kind, rustic furniture visually loses volume while dark colors allow it to gain in presence.

48

NATURAL PIGMENTS

With no more than one or two new elements, we can give a completely different air to a space. Natural pigments permit us to obtain much more intense colors. By applying the technique of draping, we can also obtain different tones of the same color. The natural fabrics in their natural colors really stand out over this backdrop. To finish off the composition, it has been enough to add some cushions that complement the wall. If white is the predominating color in this room, there is no reason to be afraid of using an ample color range in the complements.

SHAPE AND COLOR

Sometimes, it is a good idea to consider each room to be a work of art. In some, perhaps, monochromes dominate and a homogenous style which gives greater luminosity or makes them look considerably larger while in others, which are sufficiently spacious, we may try the contrary effect to obtain more intimacy. Playing on the contrasts between colors and volumes can enrich a space enormously and allow for combinations to be made with the rounded forms of chairs and sofas with the straight lines of furniture in wood or framed pictures or the base of a candle in the shape of a jug, a fruit bowl or wooden duck.

COLOR, COLOR

Painting each room a different color, as in the photograph above, can have an original and amusing overall effect. Yellow is ideal for dining areas given that it opens the appetite.

We have to give the old furniture a new opportunity. The cupboards leave the household equipment on sight. In this way, we have a space in which we can store a large quantity of utensils, but as there are glass doors, the spaces are not overweighted and they contribute to the decoration.

TRADITION AND CULTURE

Houses tell us a lot about their inhabitants. In some there is a marked desire to follow tradition and remember the family's background in the form of portraits, inherited objects, furniture that has been passed down from generation to generation.... Also, the amount of space dedicated to bookshelves or works of art gives the inclinations and tastes of the occupiers away.

ECHOES FROM THE PAST

The mixture of the contemporary with details that evoke other eras can lead to a space full of charm. A telephone from the beginning of last century on an small oval table and a lamp that could belong to the same period leave a romantic mark on this living room in which, the rest, is quite modern.

The cream color of the walls leads to an attractive contrast with the elongated cushions in green tones and different fabrics with which the space has been visually enriched. The more homogenous everything is the more the different textures used and the changes in light that take place during the day stand out. White sofas, or those in light tones, appear to be larger and they also tend to give a sensation of lightness to the space as well.

INCREASING THE LIGHT

In spaces that receive indirect light, yellow may well turn out to be the right choice of color as it is warm and luminous. If the room is not very large and there is a preference for wooden furniture in a rustic style, it is best to use light tones as they help dissimulate the volumes. Built-in shelving is also a good resource. They tend to suggest warmth as well as blending into the background if they are painted in the same way as the rest of the room.

SIMPLICITY AND COMFORT

There are living rooms in which we feel an irresistible urge to sink into their soft sofas and make ourselves comfortable on nothing more than entering. In this way, we could spend hours just watching how time goes by. They are those places that are so unpretentious, so welcoming and that are so difficult to separate oneself from. A woolen blanket to throw on top of yourself, cushions with brocade or knitted, printed or plain, a carpet of coconut fiber, some daisies from the garden in a glass vase... Curiously, they are all simple elements, but the loving care with which they have been chosen stands out. The wide and comfortable sofas develop a particular way of being in a room and contribute tremendously to the creation of a welcoming space.

OPENING SPACES

In general, rustic constructions were not designed with the idea of excessively large spaces in mind, as their priorities were others. In the two ambiences that we can see in the images on these pages, the elimination of walls to unify two rooms has been opted for in such a way that luminosity and space have been gained.

VAULTED CEILINGS AND OPEN SPACES

A large amount of the charm that a rustic house has lies in its structure and in the materials that it has been made of. Arches and vaulted ceilings offer a sensation of amplitude that balances the great weight of the stone, wood or clay. Some nonstructural walls have been eliminated to gain natural light and to communicate the different ambiences within the same room. From a visual point of view, the space has been lightened in weight by the white sofas and armchairs which give more luminosity and are easy to combine with the tones of the floor, walls and ceilings. When it comes to large areas, the decorative elements have to be of dimensions that are proportional to the whole so that we do not run the risk of them going unnoticed.

around the table

Around the cooking pots, among the clinking and chinking of plates and cutlery, beats the heart of the home. Meals are social occasions par excellence: they make us more communicative and favor negotiation and comprehension. Around the table, we gather up the energy we need for the rest of the day during breakfast, we enjoy lunch and the over dinner chatting on our days off, we celebrate traditions, birthdays.... Any excuse is a good one to try new dishes, autochthonous or from far away lands, which take us off to other worlds without the necessity of traveling.

What we will see in the following are traditional dining rooms that form part of the kitchen or living room, or perhaps, those that are entirely independent. They all have in common one of the most basic, simple and indispensable pieces of furniture: the table. With rustic airs, of solid wood, they are elements with a weighty aspect. Depending on the simplicity of their finishes and their tones, they will stand out more or less within the area.

It is the moment to recover those elements that are so full of charm such as larders, cupboards with netting, sideboards with glass doors, glass cases, which visually lighten the spaces and fill them with warmth. This is one of the pleasantest areas to fill with accessories and complements: tablecloths in white, cushions and handkerchiefs in printed or checked materials, glass flasks, porcelain jars, old tin milk churns, dried aromatic plants, ceramic plates, wicker baskets full of fruit in season. Numerous combinations are acceptable which, in their right amount, form a harmonious composition with an informal touch.

The following illustrations show rooms that invite us to sit down over a nice cup of tea and enjoy the calmness of the night or to lose notion of time while we cook or taste some of our grandmother's recipes. They talk to us about the rewards after a long walk in the countryside looking for mushrooms or the long chats in which we put the world to right or, simply, about Christmas dinner.

A TASTE FOR SIMPLICITY

Why not keep the old stone kitchen sink although it is no longer of use to us? Below the window with net curtains and the addition of a simple candle, it turns out to be a pretty composition. In the kitchens of country houses, there tends to be room for everything: some shelves with music, books, a chest, aromatic herbs ... this space is lived in.

AN OLD FEEL

White is the color par excellence for the rustic kitchens of always whether it be with wall tiles or emulsion paint. The advantage of tiles is that they are much more resistant to the wear and tear that comes about with use. However, on the other hand, they are more expensive. Emulsion paint is a more economic option that, in addition, allows us to change the aspect of the kitchen every so often with a new color. It is also a possibility to use ceramic tiling for the working areas, which are more likely to get dirty, and paint the rest. Old furniture with glass doors tends to lighten these spaces as well as being very decorative.

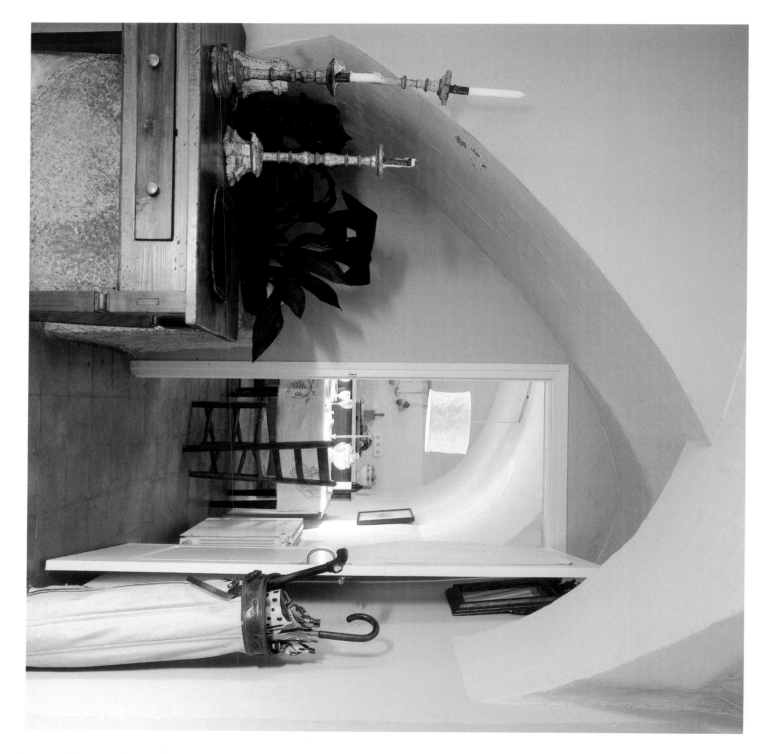

CHANDELIERS AND PORCELAIN

Details such as chandeliers and porcelain give a touch of distinction to any space. The dining room in the image on the right could perfectly belong to an English house in which the crockery and china plates become decorative elements with a great elegance. The wooden shelf situated on the edge of the change in height of the ceiling takes away importance from this volume.

LIGHT AND VITALITY

Yellow fills our house with light and joy. In addition, it often turns out to be the right choice for dining rooms and kitchens, as this color tends to open up our appetites. Orange, on the other hand, is not as luminous, but it is full of energy and it creates very warm spaces. In the kitchens, in which new electrical appliances have to coexist with the original structures, it is important to obtain a balanced fusion between the modern and old elements to create a welcoming atmosphere that adapts to our needs as well as allowing us to enjoy the functionality of the new and the charm of furniture with a history at the same time. The wooden beams, the glass cabinets with porcelain elements along side an extractor and aluminum lamp form an attractive contrast.

COOL COLORS

Mauve and green increase the light in any space and they are also cool relaxing colors. Some freshly picked flowers of the same tones will strengthen this effect. If we wish to distract visual weight from the wooden beams or the pieces of furniture, a good solution is to paint them all in light colors which will also give a sense of great luminosity and amplitude.

A lamp with glass tears gives the dining room a refined classical touch that contrasts with the rustic structure of the whole. Some small details such as the chandeliers or a series of pictures follow the same criteria.

RICH TABLE LINEN

Some simple white tablecloths and covers for the chairs dress the space in an elegant way. Over these neat and tidy cloths, the crockery and glasses take a leading role, be it that they are classical or artisanal. The simplicity offered by this monochrome in white makes these spaces seem to be timeless. In the two images, a detail as simple as a lamp seems to be able to determine whether a particular dining room is modern or classical in style.

80

UTENSILS ON VIEW

Rustic kitchens allow for utensils to be stored in all sorts of ways: modern or antique furniture, with glass or net fronts, built-in with or without curtains, larders, cupboards... there are a great number and variety of possibilities. We can even leave casseroles, lids and frying pans on view over the tiles or hang them from ingenious devices. In this last case, we will acquire an atmosphere of a more rustic atmosphere that is typical of traditional kitchens, however, toned down with an adequate use of color and accessories it can turn out to be a completely contemporary. A small oil painting, some mimosas or aromatic flowers can adequately complete the scene.

SEPARATED AMBIENCES

Bare brickwork is another option that can have an attractive result in combination with plaster and, why ever not, also with tiles. If there is a large variety of materials and colors in the walls and ceilings, it is advisable to keep the furnishings simple to lighten the atmosphere. In this residence, an arch separates, as well as communicating, the dining room and kitchen.

the Arabian nights

Night falls. The house lights are put out one by one. We deserve the reward of rest and sleep. Once again we are granted the gift of being able to snuggle up between clean sheets and on soft pillows and of being able to abandon body and soul to rest, to fantasize, to the world of dreams that comes to life when we sleep.

We are in the night zone of the home, the most intimate. It is the moment of silence and whispers as well as that of dedicating a little time to ourselves in the ritual that precedes our rest. Why not wallow in a bath of hot water with salts or bubbles? Relax in steam and, after, feed our skin and spirit with oils and perfumes. These baths, which we propose, form an inseparable part of the master bedroom. They maintain pieces of the house's original sanitaryware, restored with loving care, set alongside other new pieces which reproduce the old bathroom styles.

In the bedroom, special attention is paid to the fabrics in the form of curtains or bedspreads. Fabrics dress the rooms and, to a great extent, define their characters. Cotton, natural silk, wool or viscose, brocade, printed or in plain colors…, we have, at our disposal, a wide range of possibilities to give warmth and character to the different spaces. The ambiences that we have selected offer a multitude of ideas when it comes to furniture and accessories. They are welcoming and thought-provoking ambiences which on occasions seem to have been taken out of fairy tales.

We will see models with solid headrests and others that have been worked with marquetry, rounded forms, straight ones, scrolls, with moldings or in forged steel. Some have made that dream from infancy of sleeping under a canopy come true. How inviting the matching gauze is! The mosquito nets are also suggestive accessories. They talk to us about far distant countries and of adventures… they give an overall colonial air. A wide range of possibilities exist: leave room for creativity in what will be our most intimate corner.

MORNING SUN

The best orientation for the bedrooms is east, as this allows us to enjoy the first light of the day. The use of light colors for the walls and bedspreads will reinforce this aspect. Additionally, a soft color scheme will give a greater sense of amplitude which makes it especially recommendable for reduced spaces. If the room is small, it is also a good idea to use steel, as wooden elements in a rustic style tend to take up a lot of room while finer metal structures tend to lighten the space. However, it is true to say that wood in light colors or lightly stained also has less visual impact than that in dark shades. Cotton, linen or silk are a safe bet because of their agreeable feel and great quality.

GAUZE AND CANOPIES

Bedrooms for all tastes, from minimal expression to the most sophisticated caprices. Some have a taste for simplicity while others prefer to adorn their beds with canopies and feel wrapped up among their fabrics like real kings and queens. The small marble table with metal legs, which match the bench at the foot of the bed as well as the bed base itself, combines to perfection to create a harmonious whole.

SIMPLE RESOURCES

Mirrors are a good resource to create a sensation of amplitude in reduced spaces, as we can see in the image on the left.
If the bedrooms are large enough, they can become our small refuges on Sunday mornings. With a table and some chairs next
to the window we can be assured of a calm and relaxing breakfast which gentles our awaking on rest days and,
when we want, conserves a little of our intimacy.

THE COLOR CRIMSON

Not all is rest. In the bedroom, there is also passion, fury... let's allow ourselves to be taken away by one or other impulse. Red is a dynamic color, the color of activity, communication and affection. Why not paint the master bedroom in crimson? With a few light-colored elements that create a contrast with the walls, we can achieve a visual composition of great force that does not need any impressive accessories. On occasions, to change the aspect of a room is as easy as this: new colors on the walls, new matching fabrics and we have a new, much more daring look.

DETAILS OVER WHITE BACKGROUNDS

In this bedroom, there has been a desire to conserve a small simple washbasin from the original installation. The detail of the border made up of four small tiles hand-painted in tones of blue catches the eye for its charm. The other decorative elements in this corner for washing are unconventional and give an informal and spontaneous air.

In the image on the right, double net curtains flap in the breeze and the white console table next to the window reminds us of minimalist decoration in which beauty is found in the subtle.

THE BEAUTY OF CONTRASTS

Contrast can lead to compositions of a great elegance. The heavy wooden beams along with the mosquito net that enfolds the bed as if it was embracing it produces a very agreeable visual effect. Something similar takes place with the light and dark tones which, each in its particular measure, dress the ambiences in austere distinction. Using no more than a handful of things such as cushions, photographs in black and white, an iron bedhead or a small lamp we can give a great amount of character to our surroundings.

FLOWERS AND STRIPES

Without being afraid of printed designs, in the top image, we have an example of how curtains with a floral print can mix with bedcovers in stripes. It is a question of trying with different samples in the room itself to test the effect of the light over the papers and narrow things down to a particular range of colors. What is without a doubt is that the result is a room with a character of its own. On the right, the canopy is discretely covered by the upper part.

MOSQUITO NETS OR VOLUTES

Mosquito nets are a practical resource and easy to fit and are highly decorative. In the photograph on the following page, once again we find the same snakelike forms in the volute of the bedhead with a marked verticality as in the small lamps. The tiny pictures that decorate the walls fit in completely with the elegant and classical style of the room.

SPOIL YOURSELF

Canopy or bedhead with volutes? Silk or linen? Oriental print or Venetian fabrics? In the bedrooms, more than in any other place in the house, is where we can allow these caprices that give such a personal touch to our surroundings. In this intimate space, we must let our imagination loose and play with different colors, forms, fabrics and styles. If we like the result, it will all be perfectly justified.

If the bathroom communicates with the bedroom, it is preferable that it follows the same line although questions such as the color of the walls offer various possibilities. It depends on whether we want to present them as different spaces or as one being the extension of the other.

BEDSPREADS THAT STAND OUT

A bedcover with a print in eye-catching colors becomes the center of attention in some bedrooms such as the one in the image that we can see over these lines. The decoration of the beds allows for many possibilities that we can vary on a day to day basis. Cushions, pillow slips, sheets which are partially on view, a blanket or a plaid over the feet, a handkerchief . . . any small detail will bring about a change in the appearance of this piece of furniture and with it, one in the overall aspect of the room.

The light from a lantern such as the one in the image on the following page creates a special and romantic atmosphere.

FAITHFUL TO THE ORIGINAL.
The washbasin and faucets are faithful to the original style of the house. These sanitary fittings of an antique style combine to perfection with the charming details such as the fitted net curtains in the window. A few well-chosen elements manage to create a homely atmosphere in which the antique mirror in a gilded frame particularly stands out.

A warm and welcoming bedroom thanks to the combination of the color scheme and the materials used. The wood, present in the furniture, beams, ceilings and windows, makes a considerable contribution to creating this cozy effect.

A ROMANTIC TOUCH

There are things that are never out of fashion and that have had the same effect for as long as we can remember. There is nothing more romantic than a red rose in the light of a candle that leaves nothing to say. In the photograph on the right, the combination of red and white in small doses has also been used. The result is elegant and cheerful. The winged armchair next to the window promises long hours of reading in complete intimacy.

A REFUGE TO DREAM IN

Blue is the color of dreams, of amplitude, of the infinite. This bedroom seems to have been dug out of the ground like a burrow in which a mother warms and protects her litter. The vaulted stone walls produce a sensation of narrowness, however, the use of blue in the bedspread and cushions has been a good choice of color to achieve a greater sensation of space. Small details such as the oil lamp on the bedside table complete this dreamlike atmosphere. The small tiles along with their borders with geometric designs in blue dress the walls with a classical elegance. Printed curtains in the same colors hide the storage space located below the marble handbasin.

OTHER LANDS

Travelers or dreamers, the owners of these bedrooms doubtlessly appreciate the brilliance of whitewashed Mexican walls and the colorful cloths or rich fabrics from the East. In both cases, it has been decided to introduce this ethnic air in small doses. The result is a great luminosity and rooms full of joy in which, more than showing, things are suggested.

CLASSICAL STYLES FROM HERE AND THERE

These bedrooms are both examples of classical styles, but with a very different decoration in each case. The image on the left takes us off to a traditional Mexican house. The small lace tablecloth that covers the bedside table and the small candleholder strengthens the style. In the photograph on the following page, on the other hand, the bedclothes follow a much more electric line.

116

BASIC COLORS

Blue and yellow are colors that are easy to combine. In these two bedrooms, we can see how as much in one as in the other rich compositions have been obtained. Should we wish to give a sensation of amplitude, it is best to paint in blue while if our intention is to strengthen the light, yellow is better.

an oasis for our senses

One of the most agreeable aspects of a rural residence is the binomial indoor/outdoor life. Being able to enjoy the open air while being at home is a privilege. In the same way, it really is a luxury to be able to make the most of sunny winter days to recharge with energy and vitality. If, in addition, we are comfortably sat among cushions on wickerwork chairs taking an aperitif while contemplating the views, we can feel that we have found our little paradise here on earth.

These instants of contemplative life turn out to be so pleasurable, so far away from the stress of the city, from the noise and the hurries... Beyond the peace and quiet that we find in the natural environment, we are invaded by nature's visual show which transforms day by day and season after season. And in the middle of these bursts of forms, light, color and life, we humanize the landscape so that it accommodates us and protects our intimacy.

The exteriors that we have selected show a great variety of styles. There are those with an oriental influence or which follow a more Mediterranean line, with romantic airs, colonial or with a pronounced rustic touch. Each house, each garden offers a very particular way in which to live inside or outside. Some have pergolas crowned with creeping grapevines, porches under which to shelter from the summer sun and, on the other hand, others that have no sort of roofing at all.

Whatever the case, the design of the changes that we wish to introduce to adapt things to our tastes and necessities is fundamental. Split cane, bamboo and fabrics or blinds may be just the job to create a small shaded area outside. Carpets made of natural fibers are also a good complement with which to create welcoming spaces. In the open, decorative elements tend to be at a minimum, as the vegetation does not allow for much competition.

In the exterior zones, be they gardens, terraces or patios, we see various ambiences that, on occasions, belong to the same home. While some have been devised to animate conversation in small groups, others are based around a table or oriented toward the horizon be it sea or mountain, and there are also those which, thanks to hammocks or hybrids between beds and sofas, one can go from reading to sleeping without moving.

BEDS FOR OUTSIDE

Why not install a bed next to the swimming pool? After a dip we can enjoy the sun in the most comfortable way that exists and snooze while we dry ourselves in the heat of the sun.

When it comes to eating, we may prefer to shelter under a ceiling of briar. Some curtains help complete the shady area and can remain open or closed according to the degree of intimacy or light that we desire.

LOOKING OUT TO SEA

It is difficult to compete with the beauty of a natural landscape. In the corners in the open air, it is the vegetation, the sea and the distant mountains that stand out. To be able to enjoy the views of a distant horizon has a very positive influence on the character. Who can live without the sun, water and air? In our private photosynthesis, we transform it into vitality and optimism.

In the hot days of summer, the shadow cast by a thick creeping plant can make us feel like we are in a small oasis. The rest zones beside the swimming pool, strategically situated below an olive tree, fulfil the same function as the pergola covered by dense leaves and flowers.

124

TIME TO REST

An easy chair on wheels turns out to be very practical for changing situation as convenient. The landscape is the absolute star of these outdoor spaces. In spite of being an open space, the setting made up of a cork tree, easy chair and small table converts this corner into a welcoming place for contemplative life or resting. On the following page, an agreeable atmosphere in which the plants play a fundamental part.

THE ROUTE OF THE SUN

The garden invites us to enjoy the agreeable spring temperatures and allows us to recharge our batteries in winter by making the most of the sun's timid rays in this, the coldest time of the year. If we select lightweight chairs for the lawn, we will leave less visible marks than with a more robust model and it will also be easier to move it along the itinerary of the heavenly king.

Exterior furniture in lightly stained wood, bamboo or wicker, and even the presence of natural fabrics, allows us to create very welcoming corners that do not need significant accessories to make us feel comfortable.

STONE LANDSCAPES

Stonewalls, with their tones of color and relief, are very characteristic of rural houses. If the cleaning of the exterior walls in undertaken, the building takes on a completely new air which is much smoother. All in all, the marks that have been worked into the walls by the weather can be very attractive.

THE GALLERIES OF TIME

Looking at these images it would seem that time has stood still since the beginning of last century. The high stone wall that surrounds the gallery manages
to protect the intimacy of this exterior dining room and create a warm atmosphere that is full of calmness.
In spite of the simplicity of the furniture, we find ourselves in front of a space characterized by elegance and austerity. The same stone
wall that protects the exterior acts as a barrier to the entrance of natural light which has been compensated for by the choice of light colors
for the floor and ceilings in such a way that the light is extended to all of the gallery.

132

CREEPERS

Plants tend to be one of our main allies when it comes to decorating and bring warmth to exteriors. Creepers, such as ivy or bougainvillea with red or mauve flowers, grow very quickly and cover walls and pergolas and are very decorative. Some creepers offer very different aspects depending on the time of year: covered in flowers in spring, burnt amber in autumn...

ROMANTIC SPIRIT

This corner is impregnated by a clear romantic luminous radiance, which evokes the paintings of Caspar Friedrich. The decay of the paintwork and the wild vegetation that invades the walls contribute to create a very special melancholic atmosphere. They are ideal corners to arouse the past and to allow us to be invaded by nostalgia. The classical architecture with Gothic arches clearly show the marks of time in the midst of undomesticated nature. There are landscapes that are more inclined than others to create this kind of atmosphere and spirit, such as regions with dense vegetation and humid zones.

A SOFA OR A BED

Of all the different types of furniture that can be used outside, metal pieces are perhaps the most elegant. Accompanied by a metal table, the large glass vases that hold the candles and some freshly cut flowers in the center make an extraordinary group that is in tone with the columns of the gallery. In the illustration on the following page, a polyvalent element that is full of charm. Is it a bed or a sofa? Probably both things. The hydrangeas and the bougainvillea add a touch of color.

CHECKS OR STRIPES

In open air dining areas, we can use a wide range of printed fabrics in tablecloths as in open spaces there is less risk of overloading things. Porches can become playgrounds for the entire family. They are ideal for large gatherings around the table under the shade of their roofs of split cane or other materials. Should the structure allow for it, we can hang a swing for the children on one side in such a way as to create a play area that is also protected from the sun. With roofing in natural materials, the play of light and shade can be very suggestive.

A CORNER FOR THE ARTIST

Nature is an important source of inspiration for the artist. Upon contemplating these images we can almost see the writer, with his block of notes, in his world of fantasy one spring afternoon, or the painter, with his pallet, easel and canvas, painting an impressionist picture of the garden with the dense vegetation broken down into thousands of brushstrokes.

A RUSTIC ATMOSPHERE

This house conserves all of the spirit of a house in the country. Some details, such as unpaved floor and the remains of indigo on the upper part of the window frame, emphasize the rustic air of this corner. The wicker baskets are a good resource when it comes to decorating these areas. In addition to being practical and resistant, they look good with fruit, flowers or fabrics. It is important to take questions such as the orientation and the shady zones into account when it comes to designing the different areas of the garden. In summer, we appreciate the dining area being orientated toward the north or west.

BEAUTIFUL ITALY

These illustrations take us off to a spot in Tuscany. The reddish walls have gained in beauty thanks to the particular landscape that water and time have painted on their surfaces. In this composition, there has been a play on earth tones and blue which we find in details such as the hand-painted Venetian tiles, the curtains or crockery. In this exterior space, the plants become decorative elements par excellence. We can imagine the intimate atmosphere that the lit candles create during the night in this corner, which is protected by the house, the wall and the exuberant vegetation.

OPEN AIR DINING AREAS

In gardens and patios and on terraces, the location of the table is determined by the position of the sun and season of the year. If different orientations are not available to us, lightweight furniture will enable us to enjoy sun and shade according to taste. Daisies are plants that are not very delicate and that grow easily which makes them ideal for decorating terraces.

OPEN OR CLOSED

An English garden or a French garden? Deliberately spontaneous or designed by the owners? Gardens tell on a lot about their owners and their spirit, be it romantic or rational. Looking at the illustration above these lines, we could think that we were in a clearing in the forest, in the country. The desire to conserve the rustic character of the surroundings is clear. The autochthonous plants are those that, without a doubt, stand out. In the image on the right, dense foliage completely invades the patio.

SEASONAL FLOWERS

Flowers of the season are an easy and eye-catching resource to decorate corners in the exterior. In the garden, climbing plants are good allies when it comes to constructing spaces. Helped by structures such as pergolas, arches or porches, they manage to create welcoming atmospheres that protect us from the summer sun and, on many occasions, engulf us in their fragrances. If we wish to enjoy the summer nights, a cheap and effective way of obtaining a warm atmosphere is to use candles. Despite the contrast between the points of light and the darkness of the surroundings, we can enjoy the night sky.

152

AN ARABIAN GARDEN

These are two clear examples of exotic atmospheres which take us on a journey without moving us away from our homes. Being in a garden such as the one in the image on the following page can become an authentic pleasure for our senses: the richness of form and color, the sound of the water that runs into the pool, like relaxing music, the textures of the fabrics, the mint tea and the overwhelming aroma of the jasmine...

Now, it is just a question of letting time slip by without counting the hours.

details with character

Some freshly cut roses in a glass vase can change the aspect of a room by their colors, by their freshness. The eye is caught and seduced by silk plaid in brilliant crimson draped in an informal way over the back of a sofa, or in cushions of various sizes and textures that cover a lightly stained wooden structure. Fabrics, net curtains, gauze, porcelain flasks or oval frames, "God is in every detail", as was well indicated by the German architect Mies van der Rohe. Small objects take a great importance in decoration and the simpler this is, the more the complements or the finishes of the walls or the furniture stand out. Not to mention the corners that we have visited within this book which, on many occasions, stamp character onto the different rooms. This singularity can also be found in the unexpected positioning of a piece of furniture, in an old restored element to which a new use is given or in a touch of color that breaks the monochrome.

WICKERWORK BASKETS

With the passing of time, we accumulate a great many things in our homes, which could come to be a decorative style in itself. But there are always bits and pieces that we do not like to have on view. Some wickerwork baskets turn out to be a handy solution to these problems and they are very decorative. They can be arranged on shelves or on the floor. On the following page, the combination of the stone and the blue of the painted wall creates an attractive contrast.

INSIDE OR OUTSIDE

Why not experiment with locating the furniture? An original distribution of the elements can help us create compositions that are visually surprising. Putting a piece of kitchen furniture outside in a covered area or in front of a glazed surface gives the piece a very special air. Even like this, neither the natural illumination nor the landscape loses any of its importance in this room in which the light and shade enrich the textures of the space. We seem to be in the thick of nature, mixed in with the landscape. The wood with a lightly stained finish, the wickerwork and the combination of different types of natural fabrics in light colors make it a welcoming space.

GOOD OLD CUSTOMS

The pace of modern life increasingly leads us to buy packaged products to use and throw away and to forget such details as always having some freshly cut flowers in the house. Having an attractive bottle for the wine or picking a small bunch of flowers in the garden to put in a vase on the table changes the aspect of any corner.

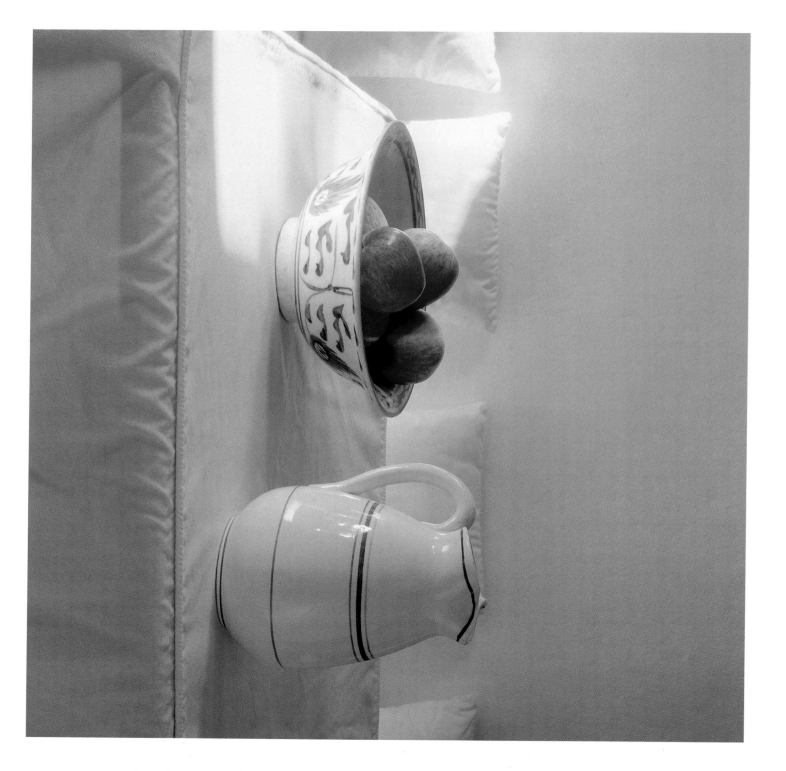

EVERYDAY STILL LIFES

There are those who say that the most important thing in life is to seek beauty and the great merit is to find it in the simplest things such as these improvised still lifes. Jugs, bottles, fruit bowls, glass or china vases are good allies. The image of the grapevine with its incipient fruit, on the following page, is the best picture we could possibly have, framed by the wooden window.

WARMTH AND COLOR

By painting walls and door to match, we obtain an attractive effect in the rooms. In the illustration over these lines,
the profiles in yellow and red are details that attract our attention.
In the image on the right, an autumn scene. The seasons also effect the home:
a few leaves are enough to bring autumn into our living room.

GREEN IVY

Ivy is a plant that quickly covers walls. It is the same throughout the year, very resistant and it is only
necessary to shape it a little every now and then.
On the following page, some details of freshness: bitter apples
in a small basket and some leaves.

BEDHEADS FROM OTHER TIMES

With these airs of times past, iron bedheads and the canopies of long fabrics take us to another age. As much as if they are of a classical style, as in the photograph, as if they are more rustic, as we have seen in other illustrations, it cannot be denied that they are not what is commonly seen. The built-in furniture gives off a country aroma and is very welcoming. In the photograph on the right, the back of the sofa and the armrests are also two shelves, or even auxiliary tables.

FRAGRANCES AND VAPORS

The bathroom can be a place full of surprises. Some flasks with oils, essences or creams, a bar of soap in the form of food, some towels rolled up on a small shelf and, why not, a freshly cut rose, a present for our senses. The simplicity of form and color is also a virtue. On this table with a natural finish, the cups that we see on the tray and a handful of flowers are enough to create an attractive composition.

ROMANTIC CORNERS

These two images could be a scene taken from a 19th century novel. A writing desk then fulfilled part of the means of communication. We can almost see someone seated with a feather scribbling on thin sheets of paper. The tray on the following page tells us about a change in language without words. Who could have taken the breakfast to the bed of their loved one, and we know because the rose tells us . . .